CW00970233

STYLE
WORKOUT

for solo violin

Studies in classical, jazz, rock, world music & folk styles

Aleksey Igudesman

www.universaledition.com

vienna · london · new york

UE 33 338

ISMN M-008-07842-2
UPC 8-03452-06204-2
ISBN 978-3-7024-3249-2

Preface

Wow, there are so many styles. And each one, is a world of its own. Are these little pieces hard? No, but they vary in the way that each one should have a different stylistic interpretation with respect to rhythm, phrasing and pure expression. On top of that, in some of the pieces you might encounter some new tonalities.

Of course you cannot be expected to be an expert at playing in all these styles after learning just these pieces, but each one offers a special taste of the variety of musical worlds that are out there. Nowadays we are able to travel across the ocean in a few hours. In most of the larger cities in the world we can buy Asian food, French nouvelle cuisine, Turkish kebabs and German sauerkraut from just around the corner. Musically, it is no different. By now we don't have to be, and indeed should not be, afraid of the huge diversity of musical styles available to us. Of course, it's important to specialize and you will find that one or two styles will appeal to you more than others. At the same time, it's always good to have some idea of what the rest of the world is about. We are, as violinists wherever we are in the world, usually accustomed to the western classical styles from our earliest music lessons but here with our 'workouts' we explore some of the musical styles that can enrich our repertoire and broaden our musical horizons.

Recommended Listening

Listening to recordings in order to get the 'feeling for a style' is a great help and in many cases vital, as it is very difficult to visit all the places in the world and find a teacher for each style. Don't be shy about playing along with a recording either, all the best people have done it! The Listening List will give you the names of a few pieces that will help you get acquainted with the musical styles covered in this book. It is not always easy, and in some cases practically impossible, to find recordings of string players performing in some of these styles, such as flamenco. Take a look at the recordings I have made with my group *Triology* as there are several CDs, each of which contains many of the styles discussed here.

Vorwort

Unglaublich, wie viele Stile es gibt! Und jeder ist eine Welt für sich. Sind diese kleinen Stücke schwer? Nein, aber sie unterscheiden sich dadurch, dass jedes in Bezug auf Rhythmus, Phrasierung und Ausdruck stilistisch unterschiedlich interpretiert werden sollte. Darüber hinaus wirst du in einigen Stücken vielleicht neue Tonalitäten antreffen.

Natürlich kann man nicht erwarten, dass du allein durch das Erlernen dieser Stücke ein Experte in all diesen Stilen wirst, doch jedes bietet einen besonderen Vorgeschmack auf die Vielfalt der musikalischen Welten, die es gibt. Heutzutage können wir in ein paar Stunden den Ozean überqueren. In den meisten größeren Städten der Welt können wir gleich um die Ecke asiatische Speisen, französische Nouvelle Cuisine, türkische Döner und deutsches Sauerkraut kaufen. In Bezug auf Musik ist das nicht anders. Angesichts der gewaltigen Vielfalt musikalischer Stile, die uns zur Verfügung stehen, müssen und sollten wir inzwischen keine Berührungsängste mehr haben. Natürlich ist es wichtig, sich zu spezialisieren, und du wirst feststellen, dass dir der eine oder andere Stil mehr zusagt als andere. Gleichzeitig ist es aber immer gut zu wissen, was im Rest der Welt vor sich geht. Wir Geiger sind überall auf der Welt normalerweise seit unseren allerersten Stunden an westliche klassische Musik gewöhnt, doch hier in unseren Übungen erkunden wir einige musikalische Stile, die unser Repertoire bereichern und unseren musikalischen Horizont erweitern können.

Empfohlene Hörbeispiele

Um das Gefühl für einen Stil zu entwickeln hilft es sehr, sich Aufnahmen anzuhören, und oft geht es gar nicht anders, denn es ist ja sehr schwierig, zu den jeweiligen Orten auf der ganzen Welt zu reisen und für jeden Stil einen Lehrer zu finden. Es ist auch keine Schande, zu einer Aufnahme mitzuspielen – das haben selbst die größten Musiker getan! In der Hörliste findest du die Titel einiger Stücke, die dir helfen werden, dich mit den musikalischen Stilen in diesem Heft vertraut zu machen. Es ist nicht immer einfach und in manchen Fällen geradezu unmöglich, Aufnahmen von Streichern zu finden, die den jeweiligen Stil spielen, zum Beispiel Flamenco. Höre dir dazu die Aufnahmen meiner Gruppe *Triology* an – es gibt davon mehrere CDs, von denen jede viele der Stile enthält, die hier vorgestellt werden.

Préface

Incroyable, la quantité de styles! Chacun représente un monde en soi. Ces petites pièces sont-elles difficiles? Non, mais elles se distinguent, chacune d'elles doit être interprétée différemment par rapport au rythme, au phrasé et à la pure expression stylistique. De plus, dans certaines pièces, tu rencontreras certainement de nouvelles tonalités.

Bien entendu, personne n'attend que l'exercice de ces pièces fasse automatiquement de toi un expert des différents styles, mais chacune d'elles présente un avant-goût particulier de la variété des mondes musicaux. De nos jours, il est possible de traverser les océans en quelques heures. Dans la plupart des grandes villes du monde, nous pouvons déguster juste au coin, à la fois des mets asiatiques, la Nouvelle Cuisine française, le kebab turc et la choucroute allemande. Il en est de même pour la musique. Compte tenu de l'immense variété des styles musicaux à notre disposition, nous ne devons plus hésiter à les approcher. Naturellement, il est important de se spécialiser et tu constateras que l'un ou l'autre style te convient mieux que les autres. Mais il est enrichissant aussi de savoir ce qui se passe dans le reste du monde. Nous, les violonistes dans le monde entier, sommes normalement habitués au style classique de l'occident depuis notre plus jeune âge, mais ici, dans ces exercices, nous découvrirons certains styles musicaux qui viendront enrichir notre répertoire et élargir nos horizons musicaux.

Conseils d'ecoute – exemples

Pour développer une intuition pour un style, il est très utile d'écouter des enregistrements et souvent, c'est notre seul recours, car il est difficile de se rendre partout dans le monde, et de trouver un professeur différent pour chaque style. Il n'est pas honteux de jouer en s'accompagnant d'un enregistrement – nombre de grands musiciens l'ont fait ! Dans la liste des enregistrements proposés tu trouveras les titres de quelques pièces qui t'aideront à te familiariser aux styles musicaux de cet album. Il n'est pas toujours facile et, dans certains cas, même impossible, de trouver des enregistrements de cordes jouant le style respectif, le Flamenco, par exemple. A ce sujet, écoute l'enregistrement de mon groupe, *Triology* – il comprend plusieurs CDs, chacun d'entre eux reprend plusieurs des styles présentés ici.

Contents • Inhalt • Table des matières

6

Listening List

Classical

Classical: Mozart, Violin Concerto No. 3 (Julian Rachlin – Mozart & Brahms
  Violin Concertos)

Romantic: Brahms, Violin Concerto in D Major Op. 77 ((Julian Rachlin –
  Mozart & Brahms Violin Concertos)

Waltz: Johann Strauß, 1992 New Year's Concert (Carlos Kleiber conducts
  the Vienna New Years Concert)

Baroque: J. S. Bach, Goldberg Variations (Glenn Gould – Bach, Goldberg Variations)

Contemporary: Shostakovich, Violin Concertos (David Oistrakh –
  Schostakovich violin concertos)

Jazz & Rock

Bebop: *The Bird* from *Charlie Parker, Now's the Time*

Rock: *Smoke on the Water* from *Deep Purple, Very Best of*

Latin Jazz: *Luna Latina (Nestor Torres)* from *Luna Latina, The best of Latin Jazz –
  The New Generation*

Blues: *Blues Boys Tune* from *B.B. King, Blues on the Bayou*

Swing: *Minor Swing* from *Didier Lockwood, Tribute to Grappelli*

World & Folk 1: European Traditions

Austrian: *Tiroler Bergbauernharfenjodlerwaltzer (Tyrolian Hillfarmer-
  harpyodellingwaltz)* from *Triology, Around the World in 77 Minutes*

Italian: *Tarantella Pezca* from *Antonio Infantina, Tarantella Tarantata*

Bulgarian: *Sofia – Istanbul* from *Triology, Around the World in 77 Minutes*

Irish: *Morrison's Jig* from *Triology, Who killed the Viola Player?*

Flamenco: *El Tempul (Paco de Lucia)* from *Triology, Who killed the Viola Player?*

World & Folk 2: The Wider World

Chinese: *Blue little Flower* from *String Road Journeys, When Strangers Meet*

Bluegrass: *Buckner's Breakdown* from *Aubrie Haynie, Bluegrass Fiddle Album*

Klezmer: *A little Jewish Song* from *Triology, Who killed the Viola Player?*

Indian: *Who's to Know?* from *Shankar, Who's to Know?*

Arabic: *Thio Mbaye* from *Triology, Around the World in 77 Minutes*

Classical

I have written these five pieces to provide a glimpse into the various classical styles of western music.

Ich habe diese fünf Stücke geschrieben, um einen Einblick in die unterschiedlichen klassischen Stile westlicher Musik zu geben.

J'ai composé ces cinq pièces pour transmettre un aperçu des différents styles classiques de la musique occidentale.

My Name is Mozart

Mein Name ist Mozart • Mon nom est Mozart

CLASSICAL • KLASSIK • CLASSIQUE

Wolfgang visited me in a dream and said: 'Prepare your fingers in bars 4, 8, 20 and 23 before you play!' He also mentioned that this piece should be played delicately, but with a full sound.

Wolfgang hat mich heute im Traum besucht und gesagt: „Bereite deine Finger in den Takten 4, 8, 20 und 24 vor, bevor du spielst!" Er hat außerdem gemeint, dass dieses Stück zart, aber trotzdem mit vollem Klang gespielt gehört.

J'étais en train de rêver lorsque Wolfgang est venu me rendre visite et m'a dit: « dans les mesures 4, 8, 20 et 23, prépare tes doigts avant de commencer à jouer ! » Il a également ajouté que ce morceau doit être joué délicatement, mais avec un son énergique.

Universal Edition   UE 33 338

Sad but True

Traurig, aber wahr • Triste mais vrai

ROMANTIC • ROMANTIK • ROMANTIQUE

Although this piece is sad and romantic, you should play it with a beautiful tone and be a little flexible in tempo (rubato). Even sad things can have their own beauty, especially in music.

Obwohl das Stück romantisch und traurig ist, solltest du es mit einem schönen Klang und tempomäßig ein wenig flexibel spielen (rubato). Auch traurige Momente haben ihre schönen Seiten, besonders in der Musik.

Bien que ce morceau soit triste et romantique, joue-le avec un timbre magnifique et reste souple dans le tempo (rubato). Même les évènements tristes peuvent avoir leur part de beauté, particulièrement dans la musique.

UE 33 338

Waltz me all Day

Tanz den Walzer, Tag und Nacht • Je voudrais danser la valse toute la journée

THE WALTZ • WALZER • VALSE

One, two, three, one, two, three, you can sway a little during playing, but watch how much bow you use. If you can dance a waltz at the same time as playing, you are the king or queen of waltzes!

Eins, zwei, drei, eins, zwei, drei, du kannst beim Spielen ruhig ein bisschen schaukeln, aber pass genau auf, wie viel Bogen du verwendest. Wenn du gleichzeitig spielen und tanzen kannst, bist du der König oder die Königin der Walzer!

Un, deux, trois, un, deux, trois, tu peux te balancer légèrement pendant que tu joues, mais n'utilise pas trop d'archet. Si tu es capable de danser une valse tout en jouant, tu seras le roi ou la reine de la valse!

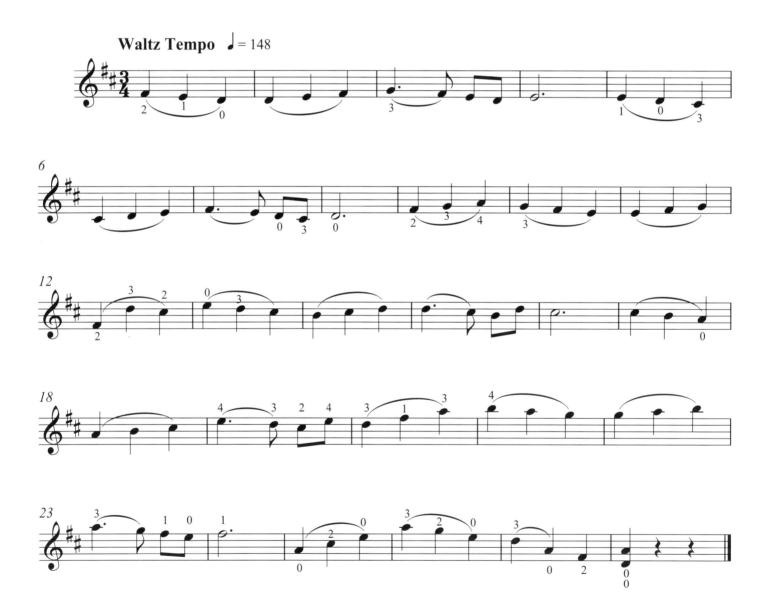

Wear my Wig

Perückenstück • Je porte une perruque

Classical

BAROQUE • BAROCK • BAROQUE

Here we go... double stops. They are hard if you want them to sound good. Make sure the bow pressure is equal on both notes. And if you have a sense of moving rhythmically forward in this Baroque style piece, you will be duly rewarded!

So ist das, auf einmal gibt's da Doppelgriffe. Schwer, wenn sie gut klingen sollen. Schau drauf, dass das Gewicht des Bogens auf beiden Seiten gleich ist. Und wenn du dieses Stück im Barockstil „treibend" spielst, wirst du gebührend belohnt!

Nous y voilà... les doubles cordes. Elles ne sont pas facile à jouer si tu veux qu'elles soient douces à l'oreille. Attention : les variations de pression doivent être les mêmes pour les deux notes. Si tu as l'impression d'avancer rythmiquement avec ce morceau de style baroque, tu seras largement récompensé !

Crazy Day

Verrückter Tag • Une journée de folie

CONTEMPORARY • ZEITGENÖSSISCH • CONTEMPORAIN

Help, so many accidentals! Find each note carefully, try to memorise the position in the left hand and play it nice and loud, even make it sound a little scratchy if you like! Although this piece has to be very rhythmical and straight, it should still have a passionate and expressive feel to it.

Hilfe, so viele Vorzeichen! Entdecke jede Note sorgfältig und versuche zu erreichen, dass sich die linke Hand die Position merkt. Spiel das Stück schön laut. Du darfst sogar etwas kratzen, wenn du willst! Besonders gut klingt es, wenn du sehr rhythmisch, aber dennoch leidenschaftlich und mit viel Ausdruck spielst.

Au secours, il y a tant d'altérations! Repère avec précaution toutes les notes, essaie de les mémoriser de la main gauche et joue le morceau bien fort, voire en grattant la corde si tu en as envie! Bien que ce morceau doive être joué très cadencé, joue-le avec passion et expression.

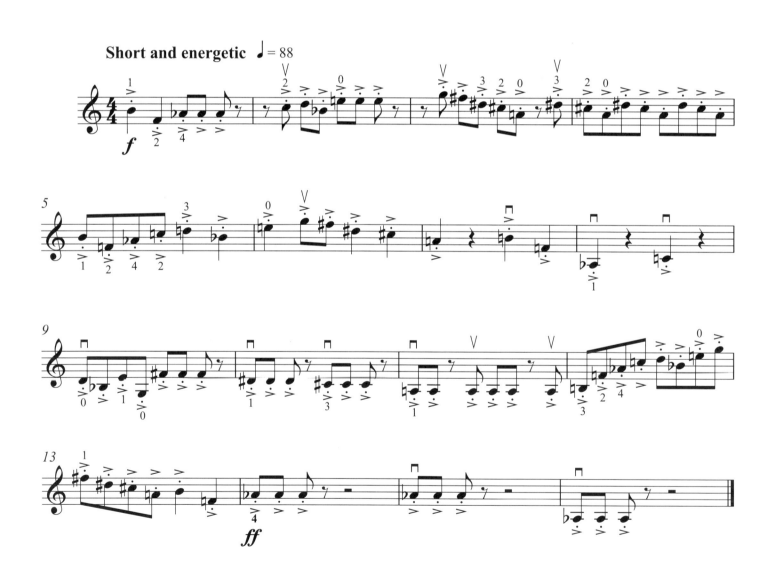

Jazz & Rock

Of course there are many styles in Jazz and Rock, but try these first.

Es gibt natürlich viele Stile in Jazz und Rock, aber versuche es zunächst mal mit diesen.

Il existe bien sûr d'innombrables styles dans le jazz et le rock, mais essaie d'abord ceux-ci.

Jazz & Rock

Cool Stuff Charlie

Coole Sache, Charlie • C'est cool, Charlie

BEBOP

If you wanna be cool, you gotta play it really rhythmically. Practise it with a metronome, man! And if you can accentuate the first of each slurred note a little, you will be the groove master. Swing it just a little bit, but play it practically straight.

Wenn du willst, dass die Sache cool abläuft, dann musst du das ganze Stück echt rhythmisch spielen. Üb's doch mit dem Metronom, Mann! Und wenn du ganz leicht die erste der gebundenen Noten betonen kannst, wirst du Groovemeister. Ein bisschen darfst du swingen, solange du ganz rhythmisch und fast ganz gerade Achtel spielst.

Si tu veux être cool, il faut jouer avec rythme. Il suffit de s'exercer avec un métronome. Si tu parviens à accentuer légèrement la première des notes liées, tu seras le champion du groove. Tu peux swinguer un petit peu si tu restes rythmique en jouant les croches de manière quasi rectiligne.

Shallow Pink

ROCK

Imagine you are an electric guitar! *Ponticello* means, play very near the bridge. This is your distortion effect. Play it straight and hard and rock all the way!

Stell dir vor, du bist eine elektrische Gitarre. Ponticello bedeutet, sehr nah am Steg zu spielen. Das ist dein Verzerrer-Effekt. Spielt das Stück gerade und hart, ihr alten Rocker und Rockerbräute!

Imagine que tu es une guitare électrique! *Ponticello* signifie jouer au plus près du chevalet. C'est ton effet de distorsion. Joue de manière rectiligne, forte et fais ressortir le rocker qui sommeille en toi!

UE 33 338

Vamos Amigo

LATIN JAZZ

Hey chicos and chicas, play this one grooving but practise it slowly with a metronome first. Be laid back, but rhythmic.

Hej, chicos und chicas, spielt das Stück echt groovig, aber übt es erst einmal langsam mit Metronom. Obwohl das Stück vom Tempo her ein wenig „nach hinten" gezogen sein kann, bleibt es immer noch sehr rhythmisch.

Salut les chicos et les chicas, jouez celui-ci avec rythme mais exercez-vous d'abord lentement avec un métronome. Jouez avec retenue mais de manière rythmée.

No More Blues

Das Ende des Blues • La fin du blues

BLUES

Open your soul, brother. Why don't you sing along to get the real blues feelin'? This piece has to feel really held back, as if getting slower, while in fact staying exactly in time.

Spür den Blues, Mann! Warum singst du nicht einfach mit, um das echte „Blues feeling" zu bekommen? Das Stück muss sich echt voll zurückgehalten – als würde man langsamer werden – anfühlen, obwohl du genau im Tempo bleibst.

Laisse-toi aller au rythme du blues! Tu peux chanter en même temps pour mieux t'imprégner de ce rythme. Ce morceau doit être joué avec retenue, comme s'il ralentissait alors qu'en réalité, le rythme reste toujours le même.

Swing it and Sing it!

Swingen und Singen • Swinge-le et chante-le!

SWING

In this one you have to be very cool and very hot all at the same time. How do you do that you may ask? Well, let's start with phrasing every first 'quaver' or eighth note just a little bit longer than the second one but without losing the beat. That's what you call swing! The metronome will help your swing to groove. Sing along to this one too, baby.

In dieser Nummer musst du echt cool und echt heiß zugleich sein. „Wie macht man das?", hör ich dich fragen. Fangen wir damit an, dass du jede erste Achtel ein bisschen länger als die zweite spielst, aber ohne das Tempo zu verlieren. Das nennt man dann Swing! Das Metronom hilft dir, deinen Swing auch zu grooven. Auch bei diesem Stück kannst du mitsingen, Baby!

Pour ce morceau, il faut être à la fois vraiment cool et vraiment passionné. Tu te demandes peut-être comment y parvenir. Bien, commençons par jouer chaque premier croche un peu plus longtemps que le second, mais sans perdre le tempo. C'est ce qu'on appelle le swing! Le métronome t'aidera à rythmer ton swing. Allez, chante en jouant, baby!

World & Folk 1
European Traditions

Here we take a little tour around Europe and look at some contrasting musical styles.

Hier machen wir eine kleine Rundreise durch Europa und schauen uns ein paar ganz unterschiedliche musikalische Stile an.

Partons en voyage pour visiter l'Europe et découvrir des styles musicaux très différents.

World & Folk 1

The Harp

Die Harfe • La Harpe

AUSTRIA • ÖSTERREICH • AUTRICHE

The chords are optional, but have a go, they are not that hard. Prepare them carefully in the left hand before you pluck them. Otherwise just play the top note. If you add a swaying feeling to this piece, you will feel like you are in the Austrian alps.

Die Akkorde musst du nicht unbedingt spielen, aber probier sie mal aus, sie sind nicht allzu schwer. Bereite sie in der linken Hand gut vor, bevor du sie zupfst. Du kannst aber auch einfach nur die oberste Note spielen. Und wenn du ein bisschen ein Schaukeln in die Musik bringst, fühlst du dich gleich wie in den Alpen.

Les accords sont facultatifs, mais il est intéressant de les essayer. Après tout, ils ne sont pas si difficiles. Prépare-les avec précaution de la main gauche avant de les pincer. Ou alors joue simplement la note supérieure. Si tu ajoutes un soupçon de rythme à ce morceau, tu auras l'impression de te retrouver dans les Alpes autrichiennes.

Spaghetti con Confetti

ITALY • ITALIEN • ITALIE

This Italian style piece should be happy and bouncy, yet rhythmic. It is a kind of 'Tarantella', a dance for people bitten by a poisonous tarantula spider. You dance until you sweat all the poison out, so this can be quite frantic!

Dieses italienische Stück sollte fröhlich, hüpfend und rhythmisch gespielt werden. Es ist eine Art „Tarantella", ein Tanz für Leute, die von einer giftigen Tarantel gebissen wurden. Du tanzt es, bis das Gift rausgeschwitzt ist – es kann da also etwas rasant zugehen!

Ce morceau italien est à jouer gaiement et bien rythmiquement, il doit sautiller. C'est une sorte de « tarantelle », une danse pour des personnes mordues par une tarentule venimeuse. Tu danses jusqu'à extraire tout le venin – une expérience plutôt vertigineuse !

World & Folk 1

Count Me Out

Rechne nicht mit mir • Ne compte pas sur moi

BULGARIA • BULGARIEN • BULGARIE

This rhythmic pattern might appear unfamiliar to you, unless you grew up in Bulgaria, where even little children can easily count uneven rhythms. Have the feeling the music is moving forward but stay precisely in time. Only count in groups of 2 or 3 quavers (eighth notes), this will help.

Dieses rhythmische Muster dürfte dir fremdartig vorkommen, falls du nicht gerade in Bulgarien aufgewachsen bist, wo sogar kleine Kinder mit Leichtigkeit ungerade Rhythmen zählen können. Spiele mit dem Gefühl, dass die Musik „nach vorn" geht, bleibe aber genau im Tempo. Zähle ausschließlich in Gruppen von 2 oder 3 Achteln, das hilft.

Ce modèle de rythme t'apparaîtra assez étrange si tu n'as pas grandi en Bulgarie, où même les petits enfants savent battre facilement les rythmes irréguliers. Joue-le avec le sentiment que la musique va « vers l'avant », mais maintiens le tempo avec la plus grande exactitude. Ne compte que les groupes de 2 ou 3 croches, cela t'aidera.

O'Reilly, the Builder of Bridges

O'Reilly, der Brückenbauer • O'Reilly, le constructeur de ponts

IRELAND • IRLAND • IRLANDE

Irish music has a groove of its own where you should accentuate the off-beats a little, but not in the same way as in jazz. Play the 4th quaver (eighth note) of each bar with a slight accent and even though you're getting a little faster you should have the feeling you want to clap to it.

Irische Musik hat einen ganz eigenen Groove, bei dem man die Offbeats, also die schwachen Zählzeiten, ein wenig betont, jedoch nicht auf dieselbe Weise wie im Jazz. Spiele die vierte Achtelnote jedes Taktes mit einem leichten Akzent, und auch wenn du ein wenig schneller wirst, solltest du den Drang verspüren, dazu zu klatschen.

La musique irlandaise a son propre rythme ; on y accentue les Offbeats, donc les tempi plus faibles de la mesure, mais pas comme dans le jazz. Accentue légèrement la quatrième croche de chaque mesure, et même si tu accélères un peu, tu dois ressentir l'envie d'accompagner en battant des mains.

The Torreros' Son

Der Sohn des Torreros • Le fils du Torrero

ANDALUSIA (FLAMENCO) • ANDALUSIEN (FLAMENCO) • ANDALUSIE (FLAMENCO)

Olé hombre! Flamenco, a music derived from the Gypsies in Andalusia in the south of Spain, is very rhythmic but play this at a speed you can manage. It can work a little slower and faster too. In bars 13–15, 18–19 and 29 throw the bow onto the string and let it bounce on the second and last notes or just play a tremolo. This will make you sound as though you are strumming a guitar.

Olé hombre! Flamenco, ein Musikstil, dessen Ursprünge bei den Zigeunern im südspanischen Andalusien liegen, ist sehr rhythmisch; spiele dieses Stück jedoch in einem Tempo, das du beherrschst. Es funktioniert sowohl ein wenig langsamer als auch schneller. Wirf in den Takten 13–15, 18–19 und 29 den Bogen auf die Saiten und lasse ihn auf der zweiten und letzten Note springen, oder spiele einfach ein Tremolo. Dadurch klingt es, als würdest du auf einer Gitarre spielen.

Olé hombre! Le flamenco, un style musical dont les origines remontent aux tziganes de l'Andalousie, au sud de l'Espagne, est très rythmique; joue toutefois ce morceau dans un tempo que tu maîtrises. Tu peux le jouer lentement ou rapidement. Aux mesures 13–15, 18–19 et 29 fais sauter l'archet sur les cordes et fais-le rebondir sur la seconde et la dernière note, ou joue simplement un trémolo. Le son rappellera alors celui d'une guitare.

World & Folk 2
The Wider World

In these pieces we take a step away from western classical music and look at musical styles
that have been influenced by it or have their origins in quite different cultures. It is essential to search
for the similarities while respecting the differences.

*In diesen Stücken entfernen wir uns ein wenig von der westlichen klassischen Musik und
werfen einen Blick auf musikalische Stile, die davon beeinflusst wurden oder ihre Ursprünge in ganz
unterschiedlichen Kulturen haben. Es ist sehr wichtig, nach den Gemeinsamkeiten
zu suchen und dabei doch auf die Unterschiede zu achten.*

Ces morceaux nous éloignent légèrement de la musique classique occidentale et nous
permettent de faire connaissance des styles musicaux influencés par l'occident ou trouvant leur
origine dans des cultures complètement différentes. Il est primordial de rechercher
les points communs tout en respectant toutefois les différences.

World & Folk 2

Spring Roll in Autumn

Frühlingsrolle im Herbst • Le rouleau de printemps en automne

CHINA • CHINE

Wise man says: If you play free in time, with lots of slow, wide vibrato and not press with left hand too much onto string, you will have happy, long life. Or at least pretty authentic chinese sound.

Konfuzius sagt: Wenn du spielst in freiem Tempo mit viel langsamem, breitem Vibrato und drückst Finger in linke Hand nicht zu sehr auf Saite, du kriegst langes, glückliches Leben. Oder wenigstens einen ziemlich authentischen chinesischen Klang.

Un sage dit : si tu joues avec un tempo libre, et un vibrato ample et lent, et si tu n'appuies pas trop des doigts de la main gauche sur les cordes, tu auras une longue vie heureuse. Ou du moins, un son chinois assez authentique.

Bombay Dream

Der Traum von Bombay • Le rêve de Bombay

INDIA • INDIEN • INDE

Let your spirit fly high and feel the peace within you. Practise glissandos and shifts on the way. The glissandos can be nice and fat, starting above the notes and sliding down into them without vibrato. In Indian music the expression comes from observing one scale or 'Raga' in many different ways. Play it freely and enjoy each interval.

Lass deine Seele fliegen und fühle den Frieden in dir. Und übe nebenbei Glissandi und Lagenwechsel. Die Glissandi können ruhig schön fett klingen, über den Tönen anfangen und ohne Vibrato hinuntergleiten. In der indischen Musik entsteht der Ausdruck dadurch, dass man einer Tonleiter oder „Raga" auf ganz unterschiedliche Arten folgt. Spiele sie frei und koste jedes Intervall aus.

Laisse ton âme planer et ressens la paix en toi. En même temps, répète tes glissandi et tes changements de position. Les glissandi peuvent être bien opulents ; commence sur la note et redescends sans vibrato. Dans la musique indienne, l'expression naît en suivant une gamme (ou « raga ») d'exécutions tout à fait différentes. Joue-les librement et savoure chaque intervalle.

Green as Bluegrass

Grün wie Bluegrass • Aussi verte que du Bluegrass

U.S.A. (BLUEGRASS) • ETATS-UNIS (BLUEGRASS)

Hi do ho! Ride that horse and slide your way through the piece. Keep a steady rhythm and you'll get home safely. You can play it a little slower and trot along or if you practise a lot, gallop back! In case you are wondering, Bluegrass is a mixture between Blues and Irish music created in the U.S.A. It should have a very rhythmic feel with a little bit of accentuation on the slurred notes.

Hi do ho! Reite dein Pferd und rutsche durch das Stück. Bleib im Rhythmus, dann kommst du heil zu Hause an. Du kannst etwas langsamer traben, oder wenn du viel geübt hast, davongaloppieren! Bluegrass ist übrigens eine in den USA entstandene Mischung aus Blues und irischer Musik. Das Stück sollte ein sehr rhythmisches Feeling haben, wobei die gebundenen Töne ein wenig betont werden.

Hue, hue, à dada! Monte à cheval et joue ce morceau au galop. Maintiens le rythme, et tu arriveras sain et sauf. Tu peux trotter un peu plus lentement, ou encore, si tu as répété régulièrement, partir au galop! D'ailleurs, Bluegrass est un mélange de blues et de musique irlandaise créé aux Etats-Unis. Le morceau doit être joué très rythmiquement, les notes liées sont à accentuer.

World & Folk 2

Oi vei is mir!

Oh, liebes Leid • Oh que j'ai de la peine

KLEZMER

Yiddish fiddling is quite something! Klezmer, a music played by Jewish people around the globe, has its origins in many different cultures. Crescendo a little towards the end of each fast note and start the next one more quietly. Like that, the piece would be good enough for Hanukkah, the Jewish Festival of Lights!

Jiddisches Fiedelspiel ist etwas ganz Besonderes! Klezmer wird von Juden auf der ganzen Welt gespielt und hat seine Wurzeln in vielen verschiedenen Kulturen. Erzeuge ein kleines Crescendo gegen Ende jeder schnellen Note und beginne die nächste Note leiser. So könnte das Stückele gut zu Hanukkah, dem jüdischen Lichterfest, passen!

Le violon juif est tout à fait spécifique! Le Klezmer est joué par les juifs dans le monde entier, et puise ses racines dans de nombreuses cultures différentes. Produis un petit crescendo vers la fin de chaque note rapide et entame la prochaine note plus doucement. Ainsi, ce morceau pourrait bien se prêter à Hanoukka, la fête juive des lumières!

The Market in Casablanca

Der Markt in Casablanca • Marché à Casablanca

ARABIC • ARABISCH • ARABE

The Arab-style scale might seem particularly unusual because of the 'quarter tones'. Basically they are flats, but a little sharper than usual – actually halfway between E and E flat , and B and B flat. Alternatively you can just play them as flats as long as the vibrato is slow and wide and the sound intense. The beginning should be very free and expressive, but with little or no vibrato. Enjoy the intervals here.

Die arabische Tonleiter mag dir wohl wegen der „Vierteltöne" besonders ungewöhnlich erscheinen. Im Grunde sind es erniedrigte Töne, die jedoch ein wenig höher als sonst sind – eigentlich die Hälfte zwischen E und Es, oder H und B. Ersatzweise kannst du auch einfach Es und B spielen, so lange das Vibrato langsam und breit und der Ton intensiv ist. Der Anfang sollte sehr frei und ausdrucksvoll gespielt werden, jedoch mit wenig oder ganz ohne Vibrato.

La gamme arabe peut paraître bizarre à cause de ses quarts de ton. En fait, il s'agit de notes abaissées, toutefois légèrement plus hautes que d'habitude – en quelque sorte à mi-chemin entre un mi et un mi bémol ou un si et un si bémol. Si tu préfères, tu peux simplement jouer mi bémol et si bémol, tant que le vibrato est lent et ample et la note intensive. Le début est à jouer librement, avec expression, avec peu ou pas de vibrato. Ecoute chaque intervalle.

World & Folk 2

The Market in Casablanca

Der Markt in Casablanca • Marché à Casablanca